The Accuro 50

A charity challenge across West Essex from Loughton to Saffron Walden

Peter Aylmer
Trailman Publications
in association with Accuro

About Accuro

Accuro is a small, vibrant local charity providing a range of clubs and services for children, young people and adults with a disability across West Essex. Our fun and person-centred services enable our members to take part in a wide range of social and leisure opportunities, helping them to make friends and develop life skills, confidence and self-esteem.

For more information, please visit our website or get in touch.

enquiries@accuro.org.uk
Tel: 01279 870297
www.accuro.org.uk
Charity no: 1094736
SCAN ME

accüro
supporting people with a disability in West Essex

 Accuro (Care Services)   @accuroessex   @accuroessex

The Accuro 50 is a 50-mile, long-distance challenge walk in West Essex conceived by the charity to link the whole region, from the south in Loughton to the north in Saffron Walden, where Accuro runs services to support local people with a disability. The idea of the Accuro 50 is to raise the profile of Accuro, and we hope to encourage participants to support the charity through sponsorship.

The Accuro 50 route guide will lead you through some of the best walking in the area, through woods and open countryside with stunning views and delightfully picturesque Essex villages. The route has a section on the Flitch Way that is fully accessible to wheelchairs and buggies so everyone can take part in some way.

Thank you for purchasing this guide and undertaking the Accuro 50 challenge. And thank you to Peter Aylmer for his significant contribution in getting this guide to press, and to our sponsors for their continued support.

Enjoy your walk.

Matthew Punshon

Chair of Trustees

About the author

Peter Aylmer lives in Sheering, close to the route of the Accuro 50. His rich understanding of the Essex countryside started young, visiting his uncle's farm in the Rodings. Since discovering walking as a young man, he's climbed many hills and walked many long-distance paths all over Britain, but still relishes the surprise on people's faces when he tells them that some of his favourite walking is within his home county.

As well as his Trailman series, Peter is the author of the Cicerone Press guides *Walking in Essex* (second edition, 2019) and *Walking in London* (2017).

Peter's website **trailman.co.uk** has details of many walks across Britain.

Also available

Trailman guide #1: The Stort Valley Way

Trailman guide #2: The Forest Way

Trailman guide #3: The Three Forests Way

© Peter Aylmer 2022

Front cover: Wendens Ambo. Back cover: Tilty church; beside the River Chelmer

ISBN 978-1-8383153-3-7

Printed by Inky Little Fingers GL2 8AX

All photographs are by the author

Mapping derived from Ordnance Survey data by Glyn Kuhn.
© Crown copyright and database rights 2022 OS licence number 100063139.

Introduction

In just over 50 miles, the **Accuro 50 challenge walk** links the two Essex towns of **Loughton** and **Saffron Walden**, the area served by the Accuro charity. It's a linear trail, principally using parts of four long-distance paths: first the **Forest Way**, followed by the **Flitch Way, Saffron Trail** and **Harcamlow Way**.

The Forest Way section starts at the tube station of **Loughton**, runs through **Epping Forest**, and then takes in the full length of **Epping Long Green**, a magnificent former drove road. Later, it runs through common land to the south of Harlow before reaching the stunning tiny village of **Matching**. The section finishes in the ancient and well-preserved Norman hunting ground of **Hatfield Forest**, a jewel in the National Trust crown.

The Flitch Way follows the course of the old Bishop's Stortford to Braintree rail line and is accessible to wheelchair users. The Accuro 50 takes the section from Hatfield Forest to the market town of **Great Dunmow**. From here, the Accuro 50 uses the Saffron Trail through the splendid villages of **Little Easton** and **Great Easton**, before using the Harcamlow Way beside the River Chelmer into another fine small town, historic **Thaxted**.

A short section of the Saffron Trail leads through **Newport** before the Accuro 50 ends with a grand sweep past the imposing mansion of **Audley End** and a finish in the picturesque town of **Saffron Walden**.

Matching

Page 1

Practicalities

Any walk of 50 miles presents a challenge to even the most experienced walkers. Though its gradients are gentle and its paths (mostly) well-marked, if you are not used to sustained trail walking, getting up the next day can be a challenge – especially if the weather has turned!

We suggest that the walk is undertaken over **two or three days**. That's 25 or 17 miles a day – at three miles an hour, nine to six hours' walking, plus breaks for food, enjoying the scenery or exploring one of the villages and small towns on the route.

But there's no time limit. **Four or more days**, or even walking short sections over a period of several weeks, are fine – especially in winter when the days are short and the infamous Essex mud at its most severe. At the other extreme, the most capable long-distance walkers will be well able to complete the Accuro 50 within **24 hours** – night navigation an essential requirement. It is not, however, designed for runners. No prizes for the fastest time.

The route's five stages each end at a place with accommodation and reasonable public transport, but many other break points are possible too.

West Essex has many good **places to stay**, from friendly little B&Bs to top-end hotels. Some are mentioned in this guide (though none are specifically endorsed by the author or the charity). Overnight halts don't have to be directly on the route – it's fine to use a bus or arrange a lift, as long as you return to exactly the same spot the following morning.

It's easy to search for accommodation either through the web or through the **Tourist Information Centres** at Waltham Abbey (for the south of the route) and Saffron Walden (in the north).

See the Accuro Website at www.accuro.org.uk/50 for up-to-date promotions and discounts from local businesses on or near the Accuro 50.

The towns of the Accuro 50 – Loughton, Great Dunmow, Thaxted and Saffron Walden – all have a good range of **shops** and the villages of Hatfield Heath, Takeley, Debden and Newport all have local stores too.

There are some beautiful **pubs** every few miles or so, many directly on the route, others not too far off. There are **cafés** in High Beach and Hatfield Heath and another near the route in Hatfield Forest.

Public transport

The Accuro 50 starts at **Loughton station** on the Central Line of the London Underground, so for many it's straightforward to reach the start. The town is also served by a bus network that ranges as far as Harlow, Ilford, Walthamstow and Waltham Cross.

There are **rail services** at Newport and Audley End, near the end of the Accuro 50, and Harlow Town, Bishop's Stortford and Stansted Airport stations are easily reached too.

There are several useful **bus services**. One runs through Epping Forest itself, to Debden tube in one direction and Waltham Cross rail station in the other. There is a good bus service between Epping tube and Harlow town centre that crosses the Accuro 50 on the A414 just outside Harlow. Also, a bus between these two places serves the settlement of Epping Green.

Further north, Hatfield Heath has services to Chelmsford, Bishop's Stortford and Stansted Airport rail stations and to Harlow town centre. Parallel to the route of the Flitch Way section there are buses to Bishop's Stortford, Stansted Airport, Braintree and Chelmsford stations – these also serve Great Dunmow. North of that town, most of the villages on the Accuro 50 have a bus service to Saffron Walden – though in the case of the Eastons and Duton Hill, this is rather sporadic.

See **traveline.info** for detailed bus times; some do not run on Sundays or Bank Holidays.

Highlights

- Across both Epping Forest and Hatfield Forest
- Unspoilt villages and thriving small towns
- A homage to the Countess of Warwick, Edwardian socialite and socialist
- Beside the tranquil River Chelmer from Tilty to Thaxted
- Audley End, one of England's grandest stately homes

Stages

Stage One: Loughton to Harlow, 12 miles / 19km	page 5
Stage Two: Harlow to Hatfield Heath, 8 miles / 13km	page 12
Stage Three: Hatfield Heath to Great Dunmow, 11 miles / 17km	page 16
Stage Four: Great Dunmow to Thaxted, 8 miles / 12km	page 21
Stage Five: Thaxted to Saffron Walden, 13 miles / 21km	page 26

Overview Map

Stage One: Loughton to Harlow, 12 miles / 19 km

Walk out of **Loughton station** by the access road. At the mini roundabout, continue onto Station Road, and then go over Loughton High Road onto Forest Road.

Loughton is a busy small town attractively sited on the slopes leading down from Epping Forest to the River Roding. The High Road has plenty of shops, cafés, pubs and restaurants to choose from.

Where the houses end, take the multi-use path ahead. It takes you to a road with a flood bank on the other side. Cross this by steps to your left and at the bottom of them turn left onto a path. Soon you will cross two footbridges over **Loughton Brook**, a tiny stream that is often dry in summer and sometimes beyond. The path rises up to join one of Epping Forest's many horse rides – these days, more likely to see mountain bikers than horses.

This ride, the **Green Ride**, is a little more special than most, for it was cut in 1882 to enable Queen Victoria to ride on horseback through the Forest, although alas heavy rain cancelled her progress.

She was due to honour the **1878 Epping Forest Act**, which safeguarded the Forest from enclosure; necessary legislation passed, with much struggle, to ensure that property speculators – one of whom was a previous Vicar of Loughton! – did not parcel up the land for housing.

Turn right on the ride; this carries the **Three Forests Way** (see Trailman guide #3). You soon drop down back to the brook, and just a couple of metres over it, turn left on a path, veering slightly away from the brook. (OS maps are incorrect in showing the left turn away from the Green Ride further up the hill.) In about 60 metres you pass a Forest Way waymarker. The path takes you up to the site of the ancient **Loughton Camp**, passing an explanatory sign just before a path junction.

Approaching Loughton Camp

It should be no surprise to find an Iron Age hill fort on some of the highest land in the area. Reflect though that it would only have been any good as a hill fort if its keepers had removed all the trees, to give a wide vista over the Lea and Roding valleys to either side. There is another similar fort at Ambresbury Banks, two miles north-east.

Keep the Camp's low earthworks on your right to a second explanatory sign. Keep ahead here, veer left and dip down at an indistinct fork in about 150 metres – if you come to a clearing, you've gone too far – and you will come to the **A104 Epping New**

Road. This was formerly the main road to Cambridge, now supplanted by the M11. It is perhaps no surprise to know that the notorious Essex-born highwayman Dick Turpin was active in this area.

Cross the road carefully and go through a gate above. Just beyond, turn left onto a broad track. This takes you into a tiny little dip, then a tiny little rise. At the top of the rise veer right off the track onto a path. Soon keep a wooden fence on your right until you come out to a road at **High Beach** [2.1 miles / 3.4 km]. Turn right onto the road and pass the King's Oak pub, an oyster bar and two tea huts.

> **High Beach** has long been perhaps the most popular single spot in Epping Forest and deservedly so. As well as the chance to eat and drink, there is a visitor centre and a field studies centre here, and even loos! Such was the pleasure traffic in the 1870s that the Great Eastern railway fully intended to extend its Chingford branch line here. Walk over the grass for a grand view over the Lea valley.
>
> High Beach retains a sacred place in the history of motorcycle speedway, for in 1928 it saw the first ever meeting of the sport in the UK; meets continued till 1967.

At a road junction just beyond the second tea hut, cross the road to gate number 62 and go through it onto a forest ride, known as the Verderer's Ride. (OS Explorer maps are in error, showing an unwalkable line, to the west.) Keep on it, ignoring left turns, to a road. Cross it and continue on the ride through gate number 36 still ignoring left turns until you come to a main road, the **A121**, at **Woodridden Hill** [3.2 miles / 5.2 km]. Cross it carefully and turn left for a few metres, then turn right onto Woodredon Farm Lane.

> At a gate, you exit Epping Forest proper, and enter its 'buffer lands' – not a formal part of the Forest, but equally owned by the City of London Corporation.

Past Woodredon House, the lane becomes a track and veers left then right to cross the M25 by a bridge. Continue on the track to the hamlet of **Upshire** [4.3 miles / 6.9 km]. Pass some pretty weatherboarded cottages on your right, cross the road and continue beside it. Soon turn left onto Fernhall Lane, and later veer right onto Long Street. Just past Nicholls Farm, look for a large hedge gap on your right. If you come to a brick wall on your right, you've gone too far.

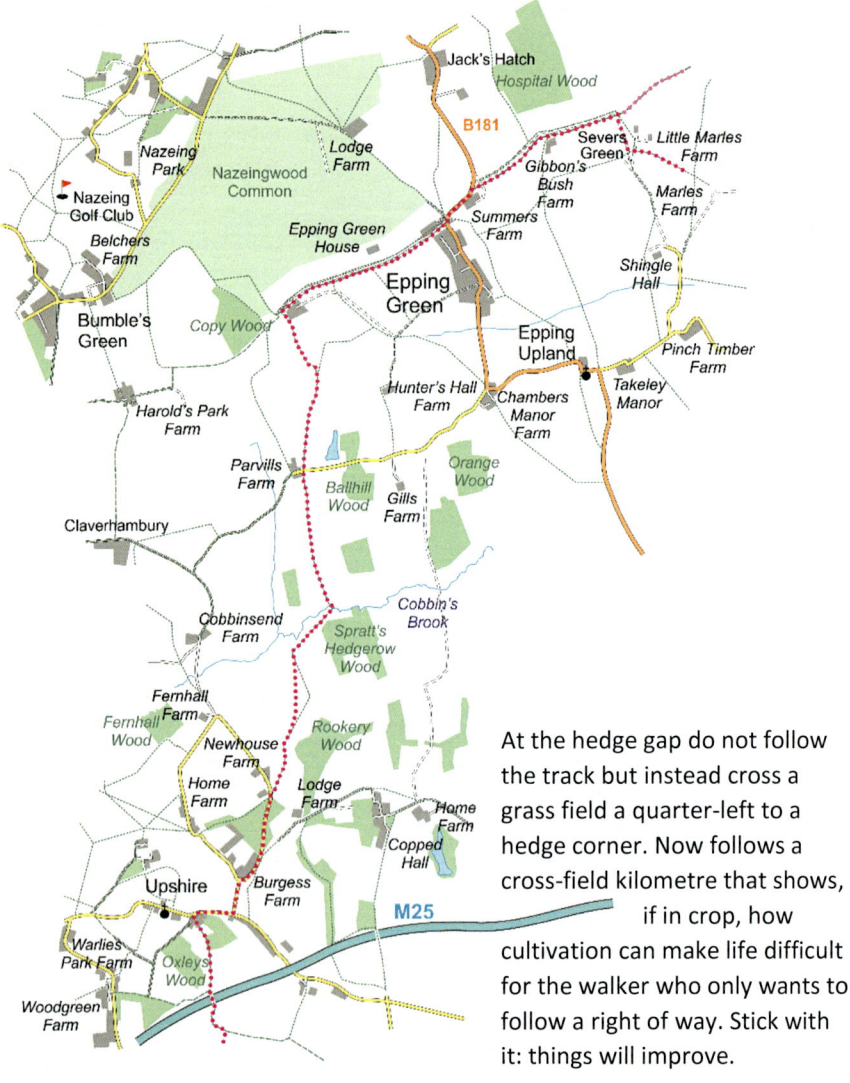

At the hedge gap do not follow the track but instead cross a grass field a quarter-left to a hedge corner. Now follows a cross-field kilometre that shows, if in crop, how cultivation can make life difficult for the walker who only wants to follow a right of way. Stick with it: things will improve.

Follow the hedgerow on your left to a marker. From here, identify the left edge of a hedgerow which has a pylon some way behind it. Your task is to reach this 'left edge'. If you can, cross the field a quarter-right to a white-topped marker just visible at a hedge corner, and continue on a similar line to the 'left edge'. But if crops mean you can't do this, stay by the hedgerow until a faint path appears through the crops to the 'left edge'.

When you reach the left edge of the hedgerow, walk beside it, keeping it on your right. At a wood corner, cross the field half-left to a marker, which marks an earth bridge across **Cobbin's Brook**. Cross the earth bridge, and things are finally better.

The Forest Way follows the headland on the left edge of the next field. You might spot a Forest Way marker in the field corner, beckoning you through nettles, but please ignore it. Through a hedge gap you join a track; look behind you here for the retrospect to London. The track passes barns to come out to a farm lane at **Parvills** [6.4 miles / 10.3 km].

Turn right on the lane for a few metres then turn left at a marker, keeping on the left edge of a field as it turns around a pylon. Go through a hedge gap at the top of the field but swap sides of the hedge at the next gap, onto an enclosed path – much the nicest walking for some time. Even better, just beyond a black weatherboarded house, turn right onto the magnificent **Epping Long Green**. Follow it for over 1km to the village of **Epping Green** [7.9 miles / 12.7 km]. The pub here, the Traveller's Friend, was alas closed as of late 2021.

> Epping Long Green was once part of the drove road from East Anglia used by generations of stockholders to bring livestock to oblivion in London. The village of Epping Green has no shop but there are hourly buses to Harlow town centre and Epping and Loughton tube stations. Less frequent buses run to Roydon village.

On Epping Long Green

Cross the road and continue ahead on the pavement, past a chapel, and soon with views north across the Stort valley into Hertfordshire. Where the road veers left, continue ahead on the eastern section of Epping Long Green. After a while you pass an isolated house on the right, and about 500 metres further on, you come to **Severs Green** [8.8 miles / 14.1 km].

Here, leave the Forest Way by following the hedgerow that veers right. As the green narrows, you come to a pair of marker posts. Turn left here, cross a footbridge and a track, and continue ahead slightly downhill through a grass meadow; then, veer very slightly right across a field towards **Marles Farm**.

Enter a field with the farm in front of you, cross it to the nearest building, then turn left on a track. At an electricity pole, continue very slightly left across the field. You will come to a marker post in a very slight dip. Keep the ditch on your right, cross a footbridge over it (many walkers just keep the ditch on the left to avoid crossing the often-overgrown footbridge), and head towards a house at the top of the field, where you turn right onto a road, rejoining the Forest Way and reaching **Rivetts Farm** in a few metres.

This route via Marles Farm avoids the busy Rye Hill Road, which has few verges, a narrow carriageway and many blind spots. The road may however be preferable after wet weather. To follow it, from Severs Green stay on Epping Long Green by keeping beside the hedgerow to your left. When you come to Rye Hill Road, turn right onto it and dodge the traffic for 1km until you come to Rivetts Farm.

A few metres after Rivetts Farm, turn left onto an enclosed path which comes out into the open at a path junction. Turn right onto a farm track, and then turn left at a path junction by an electricity pole. Soon go through the right edge of a wood, later tracking over to its left edge, and eventually veer right on leaving the wood. This brings you out onto **Latton Common**, which with Harlow Common forms a mini-green belt to the south of the 1950s new town of Harlow.

Take a grass path with the woods on your right and bushes on your left. In about 300 metres the common opens out. The path peters out a little, but continue on a line towards the rightmost building. As you drop down the path becomes clearer again; nearly at the bottom, veer right at a junction, so that you head just to the right of a prominent road sign on the A414 main road. At the hedgerow that separates the common from road, turn left onto a path, and just beyond a redundant kissing gate go up onto a metalled path and take it through an underpass below the A414.

Veer right and then left, the path becoming a road. Once out of trees, walk beside the road on grass, to a road at the White Horse pub (11.7 miles / 18.8 km).

The road to the left is called **Potter Street**, and it gives its name to this district of Harlow. There is a good bus service along the road, to Harlow town centre one way, and Epping tube the other; turn left for the nearest bus stops.

Stage Two: Harlow to Hatfield Heath, eight miles / 13 km

From the White Horse pub, enter **Harlow Common** by a footbridge beside the pub. Continue to the next footbridge, then turn half-right (not sharp right) onto a thin path until you pick up a grass track, which roughly parallels a road about 30 metres away. Do not join the road until the very end of the common, where there is a lane to Hoggs Farm. Almost immediately, cross the M11 by the road bridge.

On Harlow Common

You will be on the road for nearly a mile / 1.4 km. Most of the way, there is a verge on the right-hand side. This is the straggly village of **Foster Street**, which has a pub, the Horns and Horseshoes (12.6 miles / 20.3 km). The verge ends at a deconsecrated church, now a private house. Take care round a bend, and turn right onto a concrete track that is signed as a no through road for vehicles.

Where this ends turn left onto a road. Ignore the lane to Roffey Hall Farm and continue on the road until you meet trees. Turn right here onto a path with the trees on your left. Where they end, veer very slightly left across the field, to a path junction in a dip. Here keep ahead with a hedgerow on your right.

As the hedgerow bends left a little, look for and go through a narrow hedgerow gap, crossing the field beyond to go through another hedgerow gap and keeping a hedgerow to your left beyond. Where the field ends cross the neck of two fields and again continue with a hedgerow to your left. A gap with footbridge brings you into another field; cross it to a low hedge, kept on your right, and then turn right onto a lane. This lane, through the hamlet of **Housham Tye**, passes some pretty houses.

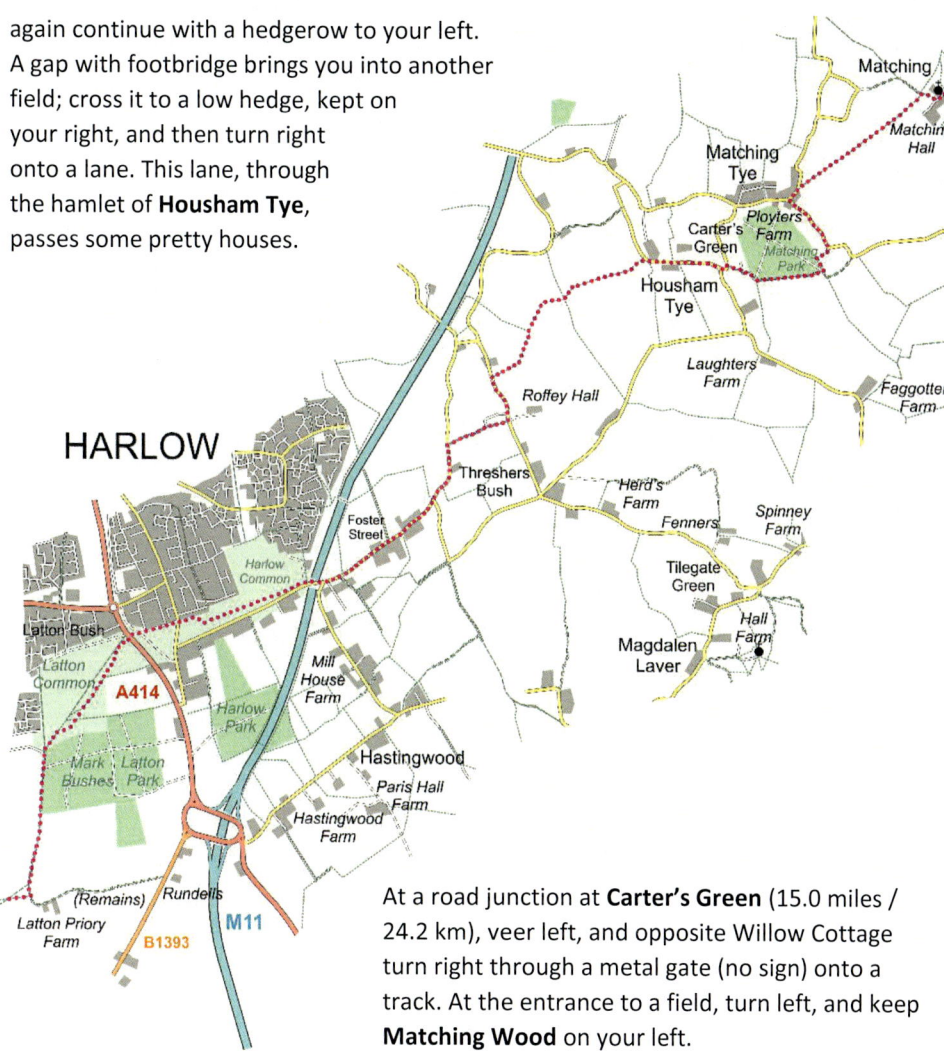

At a road junction at **Carter's Green** (15.0 miles / 24.2 km), veer left, and opposite Willow Cottage turn right through a metal gate (no sign) onto a track. At the entrance to a field, turn left, and keep **Matching Wood** on your left.

After the wood turns left a couple of times, keep on the left side of a field to come out to a minor road, following it left to the Fox pub in the village of **Matching Tye** [15.9 miles / 25.6 km]. Take the Sheering road, and opposite 'Hillcrest' turn right at a Forest Way post. This path runs without any excitement on a beeline for the hamlet of **Matching** – until, that is, you turn right to enter the hamlet itself. Suddenly, across a pond there is a near-perfect combination of church and the medieval marriage feast house, spreading oak in front, without a public road to spoil it [16.7 miles / 26.8 km].

The public road, only a lane, starts at the church. Stay on it past a pond and eventually turn right onto a road and then soon left onto the lane to Kingstons Farm. Where the lane turns right keep ahead onto a green lane which in about 1 km comes to farm buildings. Turn left to pass in front of the house before you, and then right to keep the main farmhouse, the brick-built **Parvilles**, to your left. You drop down a track.

A reservoir soon comes into view. Keep its bank beside you as it swings left; many local walkers stay on the reservoir bank, although that is not a right of way. Cross a footbridge on your right over **Pincey Brook**, an important tributary of the River Stort that rises near Stansted Airport and joins the river just above Harlow.

Over the bridge, turn right to follow the brook, and then turn left uphill between fields, soon keeping some trees on your right. Look for and follow a marker to turn right through trees, passing Gibsons farmhouse – which dates from 1400 – on your left, then turning left onto a lane.

Gibsons in winter

At the houses of **Ardley End** turn right onto a road. You come to the village green of **Hatfield Heath**. Where the road forks, take a grass path across the green, coming out to the left of the Hunters Meet hotel on the **A1060** road through the village (19.6 miles / 31.5 km).

> **Hatfield Heath** is an important route junction and it's a great place to stock up or even stay – it has a shop, hotel, restaurant, bakery, two cafés, two pubs and three takeaways. It's a bus hub too, with hourly services (fewer on Sundays) to Bishop's Stortford, Stansted Airport and Chelmsford rail stations and to Harlow town centre.

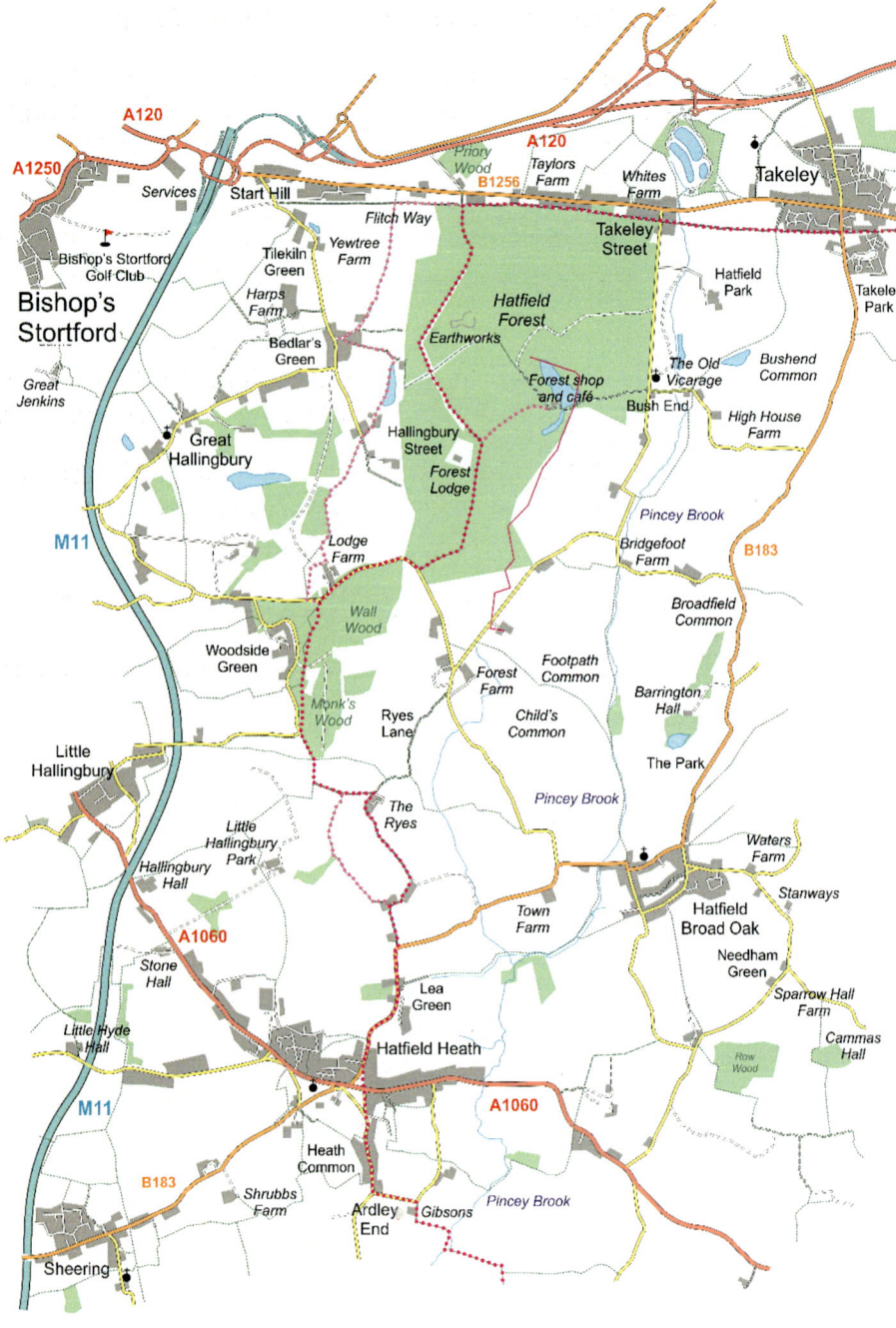

Stage Three: Hatfield Heath to Great Dunmow, 11 miles / 17 km

Over the main road, keep ahead across the green, and join a road out of the village, the **B183**. It's quite busy, but has a pavement for the 1 km you will be beside it. Where it does end, continue on grass for a few metres and then cross the road to go down Ryes Lane (20.3 miles / 32.6 km).

When this lane first turns right, leave the Forest Way for a while by instead continuing ahead on a path, then quickly turn left to pass behind a new but traditional-style house. Soon, turn right to keep a Christmas tree plantation on your left. Where this ends, cross a footbridge, continue through a tree belt, cross another footbridge and turn right onto a field edge. In the field corner go through a gap and cross a plank bridge. Very soon turn left onto a track between fields, regaining the Forest Way.

At the end of the track between fields turn right and soon continue through a gate, coming out to **Woodside Green**. This is access land, so you can walk wherever you wish. It's best to keep on the right edge of the Green until you cross a gravel track and then veer over to the top right hand corner of the green, often used as an informal car park (22.1 miles / 35.6 km). Turn right onto the road here.

On the left of the road, ignore a footbridge and the first entry into **Hatfield Forest** but take the second entry, at Gate 8.

> On occasion, the National Trust closes the Forest, for example in case of high winds, or perhaps for deer stalking. Strangely, there are no rights of way within the Forest so it is prudent to have an **alternative**. It may be particularly useful to LDWA Anytime Challenge walkers, attempting the Accuro 50 within 24 hours.
>
> The alternative starts from Woodside Green. Just to the left of where you had joined the road at the top of the Green, there's a stile. Cross it and keep a wooden fence on your right, around a corner, and then follow the right edge of the field as it curves left. (This is rather different to the right-of-way but seems to be the regular route.) Look out for a narrow track through brambles on your right, and take it. Mercifully, it's not too far before you come out into an open field.
>
> Turn left onto its headland. Just over a ditch, turn half-right across a field to a footbridge, and cross it to enter a meadow, keeping to its left hand edge. Leave the meadow by a stile in front of one of the most chocolate-boxy

> cottages in Essex, turn left then immediately right, and continue along a lane headed for Marston Farm. Just past 'The Forge', cross a footbridge, and continue on a path which later has a fishing lake on your right. At the end of the lake go through a gate, continue to a shed, and turn left onto a lane. Just before the old village pump, turn right onto another lane, shown by a concrete signpost.
>
> About 80 metres along the lane, veer left at a junction. Past houses, this becomes a fieldside path. Go through the second gap on the left and continue with the hedge on the right. Where the field ends, go through a gap and turn right onto the Flitch Way. In about one-third of a mile / 500 metres you will join onto the main route of the Accuro 50, that has traversed Hatfield Forest.

The main route from Gate 8 goes ahead on a track with concrete for an old wheelbase, which soon becomes a grass track. This develops into a broad forest ride. You will merge onto a gravel track. About 150 metres along it, just before it takes a slight right/left S-bend, take a path heading half-left across the grass.

> To visit the Forest café, stay on the gravel track a few metres further and then veer right on a grass path. It's just beyond a car park, 0.4 miles / 650 metres from where you left the Forest Way. Check on the National Trust website for opening hours.

The path from the gravel track becomes a forest ride with ditches (often clogged) to your left and right. Continue ahead at two crossroads of rides. Immediately after the second, the ride veers to the right. Ignore all side paths until you come out into a small clearing where you veer left onto another prominent forest ride.

The trees thin out a little. Don't get tempted to follow the tree line to your left but instead merge onto a grass path that veers a little to the right. Shortly beyond an oak tree you will see a gate in front of you. When you reach it, the Forest Way section of the Accuro 50 is complete. It's very nearly half the distance at 24.6 miles / 39.6 km.

Go through the gate and turn right onto a broad track. You are now on the **Flitch Way**, a trail that runs along most of the former Bishop's Stortford to Braintree rail line, which closed to passengers in 1952 and freight in 1971. This section is accessible to wheelchair users right up to where the Accuro 50 meets the A120; a distance of 4½ miles.

If you turn left instead of right, then in just under a mile you will come to the western end of the Flitch Way at Start Hill, just 200 metres from Accuro's head office. And if you go straight ahead instead of joining the Flitch Way at all, you reach the busy B1256, which runs along the route of the old Roman Stane Street. There are bus stops here for Bishop's Stortford and Stansted Airport.

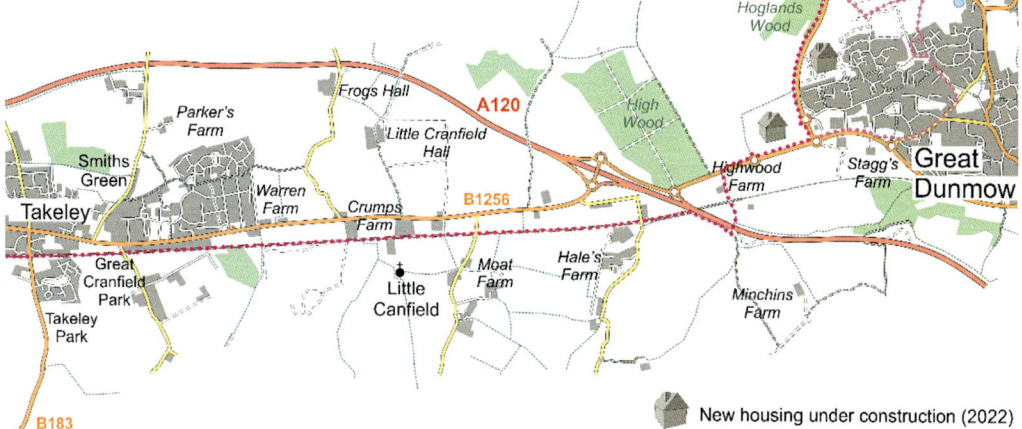

You stay on the old trackbed for 4.6 miles / 7.3 km, until you reach the embankment that carries the dual carriageway **A120** road. Just under a mile along, you pass the re-created Stane Street Halt, and in a further mile the old Takeley station (26.4 miles / 42.5 km).

Takeley is a large village and if you leave the Flitch Way here then you will soon come to its pub, The Four Ashes, and some shops, as well as bus stops for Bishop's Stortford, Stansted Airport and Braintree.

Near the end of the Flitch Way stretch you come to the site of **Easton Lodge** station – the station house remains but its platform does not (28.9 miles / 46.6 km).

The station is the start of a trail within a trail, in memory of the **Countess of Warwick, Daisy Greville** (1861-1938). It opened as a private station in 1895, well after the line itself, to help well-heeled visitors access **Easton Lodge**, a couple of miles away by carriage-road. Daisy had inherited the Lodge aged five and, even after marriage aged 20, was more likely to be found there than her husband's seat at Warwick Castle.

The Countess was one of the leading hostesses of her day – so well-loved that only one of her five children was likely by her husband; though probably none from her longstanding affair with the Prince of Wales, later King Edward VII. But what really marked her out amongst the crème of British society was her support for the socialist cause, as we shall see later.

You cannot pass under the A120 so instead the Flitch Way veers right onto a bridleway which rises up to cross the road on a bridge. You soon cross over the old trackbed and reach the **B1256**. Cross it, and turn right on its pavement. At the time of writing (early 2022) new housing was being developed here. Continue ahead over one roundabout to a second one (30.0 miles / 48.3 km), the junction of the B1256 and B184. Here, the route has two options, one by the edge of **Great Dunmow**, and the other through its centre.

Stane Street Halt on the Flitch Way

Stage Four: Great Dunmow to Thaxted, eight miles / 12 km

The main route does not enter Great Dunmow, but turns left at the roundabout, keeping on grass to another roundabout. (From here, a large **Tesco's** is not far away for café, loos and indeed shopping.) Just past this roundabout, go through a gate and follow a path beside the B184 but separated from it by a hedge. This comes out to the road in just over half a mile / 800 metres.

> The **town centre alternative** is one mile / 1.6 km longer, but it's useful for accommodation, pubs, cafés and the town's wide range of shops, and indeed much less of a trudge. Don't turn left at the B1256 / B184 roundabout but cross the road and keep ahead by the B1256. Very shortly there's another entrance to **Tesco's** if you need it.
>
> After the entrance to Great Dunmow primary school the pavement continues straight on while the road veers right, rejoining the road just before the Jalsa Ghar restaurant. Stay on the road until you reach the **town centre** at the Saracen's Head hotel.
>
> Turn left here, onto **Market Place**. At the Star Inn drop down a lane past cottages. Veer left at a pond and cross over a road into The Downs. Enter Downs Crescent past a metal gate – don't worry about the private signs – and in 80 metres continue along a fenced footpath. Ignore the first left turn but take the second.
>
> Turn right at a redundant kissing gate, then left into The Mead, and at house 14 take a footpath which (in early 2022) crosses a grass field soon due to become an estate. Go through a gap then veer left to a life belt and join a grass path past a depression that sometimes holds water. Through another gap, continue ahead to pick up a gravel path which swings right beside trees, and later goes left beside the access road to the housing development of Woodlands Park. You come to the **B184**. Cross it and turn right.
>
> From here onwards, the Accuro 50 often follows the **Saffron Trail**, which runs 70 miles across Essex from Southend to Saffron Walden.

The direct route and the town route now join. Go ahead for a few metres, until you can take a path that drops left into woodland, soon crossing a footbridge. Just past Hoglands, the path swings left and joins a lane coming from it. At Ravens Cottage, veer left away from the lane onto a grass track between fields. When the grass section ends at a marker turn right across a field. Once across it, take a grass path to the church at **Little Easton** (31.6 miles / 50.9 km). With late Victorian almshouses opposite, this is a most attractive setting, but there's more to come.

Past the church (which has a memorial to the Countess of Warwick), turn right through the imposing gates of **Little Easton Manor**. If the large gates are closed, there is a pedestrian gate on the right.

Walk a few metres, and to your left are the pink-pargetted buildings of the manor itself, while to your right, across a lawn is a grand Essex barn now converted to a theatre-cum-wedding venue. In its heyday the theatre played host to the likes of Charlie Chaplin and George Formby. There's a tea room and bar here too – it would take a superhuman feat of stoicism for a walker to pass by, if the tables are out on the lawn in summer.

The lawn at Little Easton Manor

> The site of the Countess of Warwick's **Easton Lodge** is about three-quarters of a mile / 1.2 km from Little Easton church; if you want to see it, just keep walking along the road. The Countess offered the Lodge both to the Labour Party and the Trades Union Congress, but they declined; instead, it was commandeered by the RAF during World War II and mostly demolished thereafter. Its gardens, laid out for the Countess in 1902, have survived and are a popular attraction in this part of Essex.

Once beyond the manor, continue on a grass path to a dip, then rise a little and veer right onto a cross path, soon a lane, which comes out to a road. Little Easton's village pub, The Stag, is just to your right, but the walk turns left onto the road and then, at the village sign – note the unusual **war memorial** opposite – right onto Butcher's

Pasture. At the bottom, continue past Number 18, Homewood, through a gate and over a footbridge.

> Little Easton, plus Great Easton and Duton Hill, have occasional buses to Saffron Walden and Dunmow.

Veer a little left onto a grass path which leads to another footbridge. Once across, stay on the right side of the field to a more substantial footbridge, which takes you over the **River Chelmer**, and once across turn immediately left. Cross a stile and keep to the left side of the field for 200 metres.

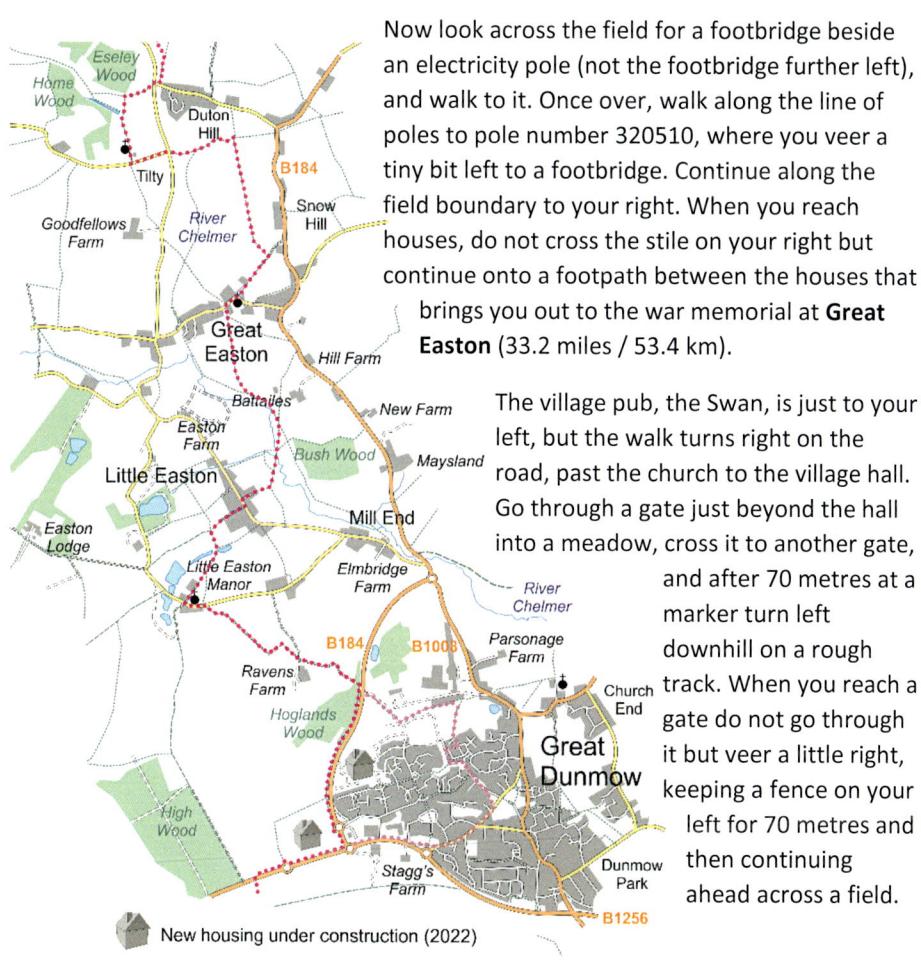

Now look across the field for a footbridge beside an electricity pole (not the footbridge further left), and walk to it. Once over, walk along the line of poles to pole number 320510, where you veer a tiny bit left to a footbridge. Continue along the field boundary to your right. When you reach houses, do not cross the stile on your right but continue onto a footpath between the houses that brings you out to the war memorial at **Great Easton** (33.2 miles / 53.4 km).

The village pub, the Swan, is just to your left, but the walk turns right on the road, past the church to the village hall. Go through a gate just beyond the hall into a meadow, cross it to another gate, and after 70 metres at a marker turn left downhill on a rough track. When you reach a gate do not go through it but veer a little right, keeping a fence on your left for 70 metres and then continuing ahead across a field.

In a dip turn left, and continue on the right-hand side of two fields to a footbridge over the Chelmer. Over it, go half-right to a stile and come out to a road junction. Take the road to **Tilty Church**, turning right at houses to reach it.

> The Countess of Warwick had the right of patronage at local parishes, Tilty being one. To promote her socialist views, she placed former boilermaker Edward Maxted here as vicar in 1908. He promptly set about preaching the socialist cause in the church, the village and Dunmow too – in return, some of the townsfolk burned his effigy on Guy Fawkes' Night the following year. He worked hard for local farm workers during the agricultural strike of 1914. After World War I ended, Maxted left for Bristol, and later served as an Episcopalian minister in Houston, Texas, where he died in 1966 aged 92.

> The church was once the gatehouse chapel of a great Cistercian abbey; look for the enormous east window and the high ceiling with original 12th-century beams. King John lived up to his bad reputation here, post-Magna Carta, sacking the abbey during Christmas mass in 1215.

From Tilty church continue through a kissing gate, the abbey ruins on your right, to the derelict Tilty Mill. Keep it on your left and take the track leading past a pillbox disguised under an iron roof. At a marker we leave the Saffron Trail, which turns left, and instead take the **Harcamlow Way**, which turns right on a path that comes out at a minor road junction at **Duton Hill** (34.9 miles / 56.1 km). Cross the bridge – once more over the River Chelmer – but just after it take the footpath on the left, through a garden. The idiosyncratic **Three Horseshoes** pub is in the village a short distance along the road.

> We will be following the Harcamlow Way for nearly nine miles. The whole walk is a 141-mile figure-of-eight linking Harlow and Cambridge.

From the garden keep the Chelmer close by on your left for over two miles, almost all the way to Thaxted. There's just one road to be crossed, at Follymill. Eventually, the **B1051** comes in from the left – where it does so, the Chelmer heads north, while a side stream separates you from the road for 200 metres, until you can cross a footbridge to it.

Turn left back along the road, cross it, and after Park Style Cottage turn right on a path which climbs towards the attractive grouping of windmill and church in **Thaxted**. After the windmill, keep the church to your right, and you will come out to the main road (B184) at the Swan Hotel (37.7 miles / 60.7 km).

Thaxted town centre is worth a side trip. Just before you reach the church, turn right through a kissing gate, pass a red cottage, and walk down the cobbled Fishmarket Street to the half-timbered Guildhall.

The large **church** and fine **Guildhall** attest to the long-standing importance of this attractive little town. Both buildings date from the 14th century, and owe their construction to an unexpected source of wealth – the medieval cutlery industry, which was to flourish here for well over 200 years.

The town had been important since Saxon times, with a formal market charter granted in 1205. The Dick Turpin connection, alluded to by the naming of a house for him on Stoney Lane, is alas more likely to be mythic than real.

Two years after appointing Maxted as vicar of Tilty, the Countess of Warwick brought **Rev Conrad Noel** to Thaxted. At least as radical as his fellow vicar, he flew the red and Sinn Féin flags from the church and, keen to encourage the arts, attracted **Gustav Holst** to the town. The composer founded the first music festivals here; after Noel died in 1942, Holst student Jack Putteril became vicar, continuing the musical tradition.

Thaxted Guildhall and Stony Lane

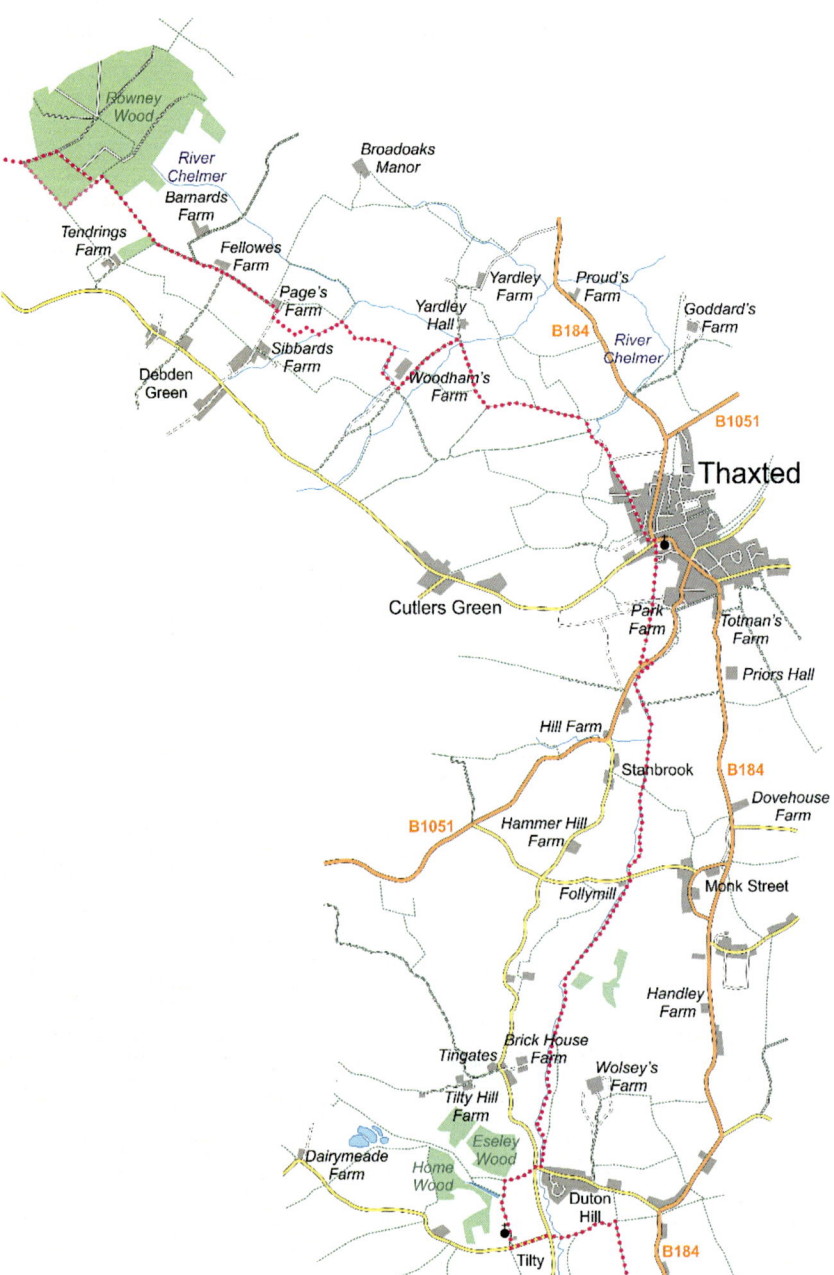

Stage Five: Thaxted to Saffron Walden, 13 miles / 21 km

Just to the left of the Swan Hotel (only cross to it if you plan to eat, drink or stay there), the main B184 to Saffron Walden curves right. There is a road to Debden, and a small lane called **Watling Lane**. Walk down Watling Lane, ignore the part of it that veers right back to the main road, and after the houses on the left have ended, continue to the last house, a wooden bungalow to your right. Some 30 metres from here ignore a gap on the right (a Harcamlow Way marker seems to beckon you through, but it is misleading), and indeed ignore the next two gaps on the right.

The fieldside path becomes a green lane. Where it ends, cross the field to a yellow-topped marker and continue ahead on a green lane, later fenced on the right. Turn left onto a lane, soon a wide green lane, and then a lane again, passing **Woodham's Farm**. Turn right beside a large gate, go half-right for a few metres, and turn left onto a broad gravel track. If you need spare agricultural machinery, you're in the right place.

About 100 metres along the broad gravel track, take a path on the right with a ditch to its right. The path bends left in another 150 metres. Cross a footbridge and turn left, onto an excellent headland path on the left side of a large field. Stay on it all the way to the furthest corner of the field, and when you reach it, turn right onto a lane. Ignore the lane to **Fellowes Farm** but take the next lane on the left, soon a green lane, which runs parallel to it.

Past Fellows Farm itself this briefly bears the deep ruts of off-roaders, but thankfully not for long. Where it turns right, look for a marker post and turn left onto another, smaller, green lane, which soon crosses a lane and not long after, as a track, crosses a field to **Rowney Wood**.

> There is public access to Rowney Wood, which is owned by the Forestry Commission. Natural woodland is regenerating here, as fast as the deer will allow it, after conifers were planted in the 1960s.

The Harcamlow Way initially enters the wood and keeps to its left-hand side, but not for long, emerging to turn left, keeping the wood on its right around a corner. This is recommended if the wood is very wet, but otherwise the Accuro 50 stays in the wood by crossing a footbridge and turning left onto a path. This joins a track; 200 metres along the track, turn left onto a path, and finally leave the wood.

Both routes now join and take a good headland path on the right side of a large field. Soon on your right you will soon see the radar dish for Carver Barracks, where many Gurkha troops are based. Nearing houses, veer right to join a lane which takes you into **Debden**.

At a little triangle veer right (unless you want the village pub, the Plough, in which case veer left) to come out to the Yuva restaurant – Nepali food a speciality, courtesy no doubt of the Gurkhas – and village school (42.3 miles / 68.0 km). There is a community shop a little further on. It has restricted hours so check before relying on it.

> Debden means 'deep valley' in Anglo-Saxon, and it occurs twice in Essex; once in the Roding Valley, one stop from Loughton on the Central Line, and here in the catchment of the upper Cam. As the name implies, some of the most undulating countryside in the county is to be found here.

Just past the school turn left down Church Lane. The route doesn't go through the churchyard (unless you choose to make a detour), but stays just above it. You come to an ornamental lake in Debden Park and turn left to cross it at a bridge. In 70 metres, the Harcamlow Way turns right at a metal sign, but instead we continue on the track up into and through a wood. Go through a kissing gate by a larger gate and veer right onto a track, rejoining the Saffron Trail (43.3 miles / 69.7 km).

> A short detour of about three-quarters of a mile / 1.3 km will lead you to the pretty village of **Widdington** and its excellent pub the Fleur-de-Lys. Don't veer right onto the Saffron Trail but take the path which crosses the field. Later cross a footbridge and continue, eventually veering right to reach the village church and, not much further, veering left for the pub. The village has buses to Saffron Walden and Bishop's Stortford.

Stay on the track for 1.5 miles / 2.5 km. There's a very short road section after Waldegraves Farm – just make sure you take the track keeping ahead when the road veers left. Also, at the high point of the track, ignore signposted paths heading first right then left.

> As you descend, there's a chalk quarry on your left. Geologically, a mile or so out of Thaxted you moved from the clay soils which underlie much of Essex to those based on chalk. They dry quicker than clay soils, so mud may be less of a problem from now on! This chalk landscape dominates north-west Essex and is part of a larger swathe that runs from north Norfolk, forms the Chilterns, and down through Wiltshire to the Dorset coast.

Newport station is right beside the path (44.8 miles / 72.2 km). It has trains to London, Bishop's Stortford and Cambridge, so it's a useful place to break the walk. The walk itself continues ahead on the road and then turns right over the railway to the village centre, strung out along the B1383. Turn right onto this road – once, the main A11 from London to Norwich – passing bus stops to Saffron Walden and Bishop's Stortford and the village shop (45.2 miles / 72.8 km).

The Saffron Trail in Newport takes a rather dull route along the main road and an enclosed, and often muddy, footpath, so the Accuro 50 takes a better alternative (but continue along the road for the two village pubs).

Just past the shop, at Bank House, turn left onto a lane and enter the **churchyard**. Walk round the church, keeping it on your right, and leave the churchyard by a gate.

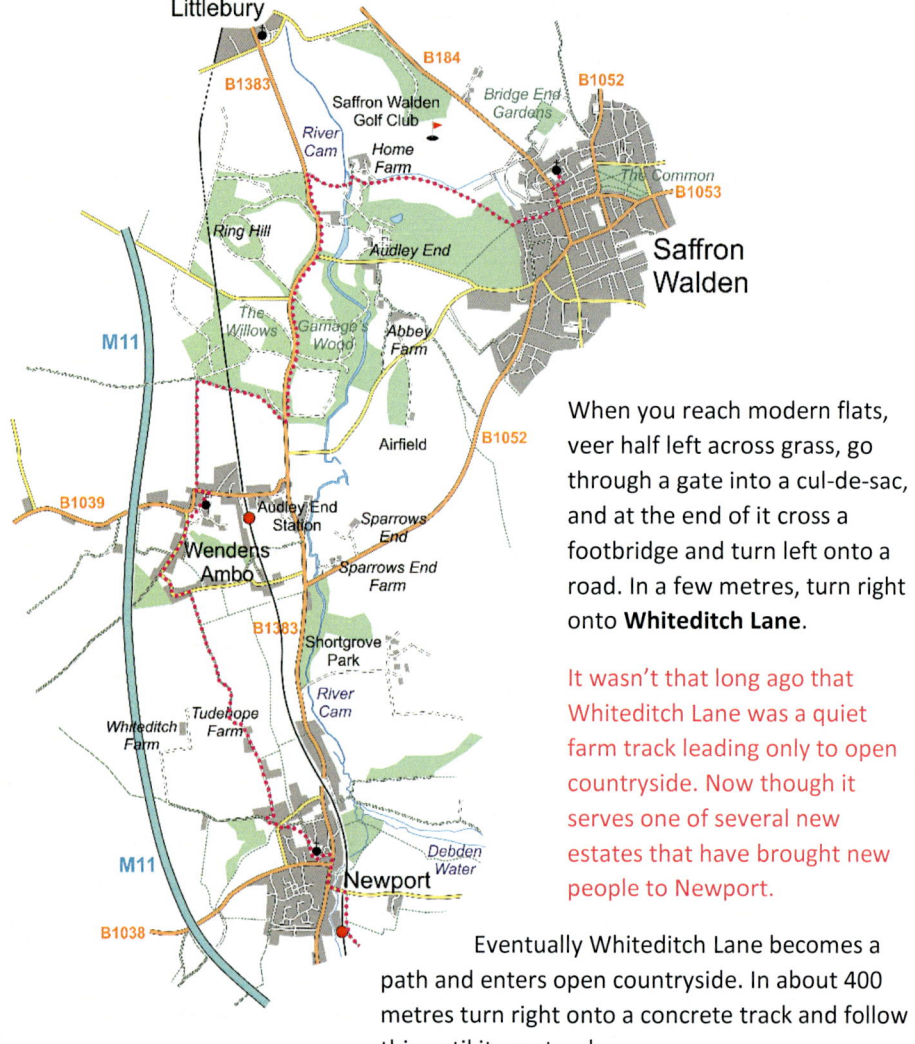

When you reach modern flats, veer half left across grass, go through a gate into a cul-de-sac, and at the end of it cross a footbridge and turn left onto a road. In a few metres, turn right onto **Whiteditch Lane**.

It wasn't that long ago that Whiteditch Lane was a quiet farm track leading only to open countryside. Now though it serves one of several new estates that have brought new people to Newport.

Eventually Whiteditch Lane becomes a path and enters open countryside. In about 400 metres turn right onto a concrete track and follow this until it meets a lane.

Turn left onto the lane, which twists and turns through the quiet village of **Wendens Ambo**. Just before reaching a more major road, go through a gate onto a metalled path in a small recreation ground. (Or, if you go ahead to the more major road – the B1039 – and turn left, you will quickly reach the village local, the Bell Inn.) The path comes out onto a lane with a row of pretty cottages ending in the church, one of the most chocolate-box views in the whole county.

Don't enter the churchyard though, but go through a gate by the last cottage. The path leads to a road – it's the B1039 (47.2 miles / 76.0 km).

Cross the road. If you want **Audley End station**, turn right; for the Accuro 50 however, turn left, and where the road bends left, turn right onto a track. This becomes a headland path. When you reach woods, turn right onto another headland path, briefly a track where it crosses the railway; after the bridge, it drops slowly down to a road – the B1383 again.

> Though Wendens Ambo is a far smaller settlement than Newport, its railway station – named Audley End – is much more important, with more trains to London, Bishop's Stortford and Cambridge plus regular services to Stansted Airport and Norwich as well. That's because it's the closest station to the town of Saffron Walden. A branch line once ran from Audley End station to the town, but it fell victim to the Beeching cuts in 1964.

Cross the B1383 and turn left on its pavement, leaving the Saffron Trail. The compensation of walking by the road will soon be clear: glorious views over the estate and house of **Audley End**. Further along the road, take the lane on the right to Home Farm. Don't go into the farm, but at a marker keep ahead with a stream on your left.

> If you want to visit the house, take the signposted road on the right, about three-quarters of a mile / 1.2 km along the B1383.

> When built in Jacobean times for the first Earl of Suffolk, Audley End was on the scale of a royal palace. Although gradually reduced in size during the 18th century, it is unquestionably one of England's grandest stately homes, following substantial remodelling of the gardens by Capability Brown, and of the interior by Robert Adam.

> Its owners, later the Lords Braybrooke (still resident on the estate, given to the nation in 1948), guarded the park so effectively that a London-to-Cambridge canal was never built and the main railway line was diverted away from Saffron Walden.

> In war time the house was home to the Polish branch of the Special Operations Executive, and a memorial to their fallen can be found in the grounds.

After the stream moves away in about half a mile, cross a footbridge and continue on a grass strip to a crenellated gatehouse. Go through the gate beside it, and enter **Saffron Walden** along Abbey Lane. When it ends, turn left onto the High Street, passing the extravagantly half-timbered Cross Keys hotel, and then turn right into Church Street. The church, and the **end of the Accuro 50**, are a little further along and to the left (50.7 miles / 81.5 km).

> The peaceful churchyard, with several benches, is a fitting place to stop and reflect on your journey. Some benches are placed around a lawn just before the churchyard proper, which hosts a sculpture, *The Children of Calais* by Ian Wolter; it comments both on the refugee crisis of present times and Auguste Rodin's *The Burghers of Calais* (1895), one of the founding works of modern sculpture.
>
> You have hardly touched on the town however. To visit the centre, go back past *The Children of Calais*, turn left onto Church Street, then go first right down Market Hill to the Market Square.
>
> The town is well worth exploring. As well as plenty of shops, pubs, cafés and accommodation, there is a Norman castle, the Fry Art Gallery which is especially strong on the works of the Great Bardfield artists of the mid-20th century, and the remarkable turf maze, many centuries old, and – be warned – a mile long!

The Cross Keys Hotel, Saffron Walden

What words mean

Some words have particular meanings in this guide.

Road: always has a hard surface, and is designed for vehicle use rather than pedestrian, unless it has a verge or pavement. If there isn't, walk facing the oncoming traffic, although at blind corners it is often safer to cross so that drivers have a better view of you (and you of them).

Lane: a particularly quiet road, possibly private, leading only to a farm or few houses. Often a dead end.

Green lane: a track or path enclosed by hedgerows either side, generally a relic of the transport network of centuries past. Essex is particularly well-endowed with green lanes, more than any county bar Dorset; Epping Long Green is perhaps the most spectacular example.

Headland: an uncultivated strip of land, usually left to grass, at the edge of a field. Essex County Council tells landowners that headlands bearing a footpath should be at least 1.5m wide, but alas some are less and in a few cases landowners deliberately scrub up headlands entirely.

Marker post: about a metre high, usually wooden, and placed at farmland route junctions where it's easy to go astray or as a sighter across fields. Be warned that landowners do not always replace them if they fall or decay, quickly or at all.

Track: not hard-surfaced unless stated, but it would be practical (though with a few exceptions not legal) to drive a 4x4 down it.

Path: usually less broad than a track, but visible on the ground. Impractical for 4-wheeled transport (not necessarily bicycles – but these are only legal if the path has the legal status of at least a bridleway), and generally not hard-surfaced.

Please be aware however that over time, development and other changes may mean paths become tracks, or lanes become roads, for example.

Crossing fields

You will often need to cross fields to follow the Accuro 50. This can be more daunting than it sounds, whether the field is in crop or not.

The first thing to be said is that if a right-of-way crosses a field, the farm owner should make it distinct. When in crop, that means cutting a line for walkers. When ploughed, that means making the line of the right-of-way clear (say, by running the tractor up and down the route a couple of times) within two weeks of ploughing. Good farmers do both. Some farmers do so late; a few, not at all. What to do then?

First of all, if a right-of-way is obscured or blocked, you have a legal right to follow it, and to remove any obstruction that may prevent you.

The Accuro 50 follows rights of way almost throughout. There is *de facto* right of access in the woodlands around Harlow, and the two Commons shortly after are access land, as is Woodside Green. Waymarks sensibly encourage all walkers follow the farm track to Latton Priory Farm rather than attempt the right-of-way across the field. North of Duton Hill, the right-of-way is technically away from the Chelmer rather than beside it, but local usage follows the river.

While in the author's experience deliberate blockage of the Accuro 50 is highly unlikely (and should be reported to the Rights of Way team at Essex County Council), problems from crops or ploughing can arise.

Leaving a line through crops - how it should be done, approaching Housham Tye

Growing crops can obscure a path, and in many cases it's simply neither practical nor desirable to walk through them. In that case, many walkers look for tractor tracks heading in roughly the right direction. In the worst cases, an alternative is to stick to the field headland if there is one, ie walk around the field rather than through it.

Although a ploughed field is free of crops, that does not mean it will be easy to cross! Clay underpins most of the soils of the Accuro 50; after any prolonged rain, the clag that can build up on footwear can easily double its weight. In general though, **please stick to the legal line** – your sacrifice will benefit others who pass that way.

But are you on the right line? Usually, there will be a clue across the field – a marker post, footbridge or hedge gap say. But to be certain, use a map. The maps in this guide are at 1:50,000 scale and should help, but the OS Explorer series at 1:25,000 is even better, for it shows field boundaries. Maps 174, 183 and 195 cover the Accuro 50. With a mobile phone, you can use the OS Maps app, or similar apps such as Anquet, to download the mapping.

Raising money for Accuro

The Accuro 50 was devised to promote walking in West Essex, to raise the profile of the charity and to encourage charitable donations to Accuro. The walk follows public routes that can be walked without donating, however by purchasing this guide you will already have contributed in a small way. If you choose to undertake the Accuro 50 challenge and raise donations, here are some suggestions.

- Set yourself a clear target – complete the Accuro 50 in three days for example – and encourage friends, family and colleagues to donate. Maybe this could be a commitment to a certain amount per day or per mile, or on completion.
- Create an online fundraising page; these are secure and easy to share by social media, email or WhatsApp. Gift Aid can be collected too. Accuro have set up a campaign page for the Accuro 50 on the fundraising platform 'Give as You Live' which you can link to your own fundraising page on the platform. Find the campaign at:

  www.donate.giveasyoulive.com/campaign/accuro-50

- Of course, you can choose your own favourite way to fundraise online. JustGiving is a popular choice.
- Businesses and organisations can agree to donate a specific sum on successful completion of the Accuro 50, by individuals or a team, or by match funding donations.

Most people will walk the Accuro 50 in small groups; some may do so individually. Because of the nature of many of the paths, however, it is not especially suitable for very large groups of more than about 20.